# Christmas for the Unborn

*How the Mystery and Magic of Christmas Call Us to End Abortion*

**By Fr. Frank Pavone**
National Director, Priests for Life
President, National Pro-life Religious Council

**Fr. Frank Pavone**

# TABLE OF CONTENTS

| | |
|---|---|
| Introduction | 5 |
| Christmas for the Unborn | 7 |
| Advent: A Summons to Hope | 11 |
| Advent: Season of the Two Comings | 13 |
| Advent: A Summons to Repentance | 16 |
| Advent: A Summons to Courage | 19 |
| Advent Reconciles Mother and Preborn Child | 21 |
| O Come, O Come Emanuel! | 24 |
| Rushing to the Side of Mary | 26 |
| Born of a Virgin | 29 |
| St. Juan Diego and Our Lady of Guadalupe | 31 |
| Christmas: Feast of the Incarnation | 34 |
| God in Human Language | 38 |
| What the Shepherds Understood | 41 |
| Christmas: Were You There? | 43 |
| Christmas: Season of Life | 46 |
| Choice on Earth | 48 |
| Grown-up Christmas List | 51 |
| Christmas, Christians, and Christ | 54 |
| Dr. King's Christmas Sermon | 57 |
| The Political Meaning of Christmas | 62 |
| No Room in the Inn | 64 |
| The Empty Manger | 66 |
| The Crib and the Blood | 69 |
| Christmas: Just Like Easter | 71 |
| The Advent-Christmas Season: Feasts, Practices, and Prayers | 74 |
| An Advent Prayer for Life | 78 |
| A Christmas Prayer for Life | 79 |
| About the Author and Priests for Life | 81 |

The Advent color is purple because that is the color of the sky as it transitions from the dark of night to the brightness of a new day. The coming of Christ heralds a new age for humanity, one of salvation, and indeed of adoption by God as our Father.

And so we begin another Advent under the shadow of the culture of death, as abortion continues to be the single form of violence claiming more lives than anything else, including poverty, disease, drug abuse, terrorism, and war. We begin another Advent under unprecedented attacks on our religious freedom, a basic human and American right.

And yet we dare to hope, and that hope is what inspires our pro-life work.

Abortion is not only a sin against life; it is a sin against hope. Think of what so many scared, pregnant moms say: *"I can't bring a child into this world."* That is not the voice of "freedom of choice;" it is the voice of despair, born of feeling one has *no freedom and no choice.*

It is up to us to make the bells of Christmas peel "more loud and deep" by reaching these moms with concrete help, and by moving our society toward a Culture of Life. We are inspired to work for this, knowing that "the wrong shall fail, the right prevail." Because hope itself has become Incarnate in a Divine Child.

# ADVENT: SEASON OF THE TWO COMINGS

Advent is upon us. The word means "coming" and the season focuses first on Christ's second coming at the end of time, and then on the historical reality of his first coming and his birth at Christmas.

When the year 1000 was about to dawn, people were fleeing to mountains, in anticipation that the return of Christ to earth was imminent. At the dawn of the year 2000, those expectations took a more technological twist, with fears of major computer, electrical -- and hence societal -- breakdowns.

Neither happened. Yet both moments in history remind us of something deeper, the lesson of Advent.

The Lord wants us to anticipate and prepare for his coming, not as something that we hinge on a particular date or identify with a particular calamity, but as *an ordinary aspect of our daily Christian living.* On the one hand, we know he is coming; on the other, we don't know when. Yet every moment is an opportunity to make that coming more central to our lives.

We know He is coming. "*For the Lord himself will descend from heaven, with a cry of command, with the archangel's call, and with the sound of the trumpet of God*" (1 Thess. 4:16). His return in glory is professed in the Creed: "He will come again in glory to judge the living and the dead." This will be the culmination of human history.

We do not know the year, day, or hour of his coming. "It is not for you to know times or seasons which the Father has fixed by his own authority" (Acts 1:7). As the Catechism of the Catholic Church states, "This eschatological coming could be accomplished at any moment" (CCC, 673).

Waiting and preparing for that coming is an ordinary, foundational aspect of Christian life. At each Mass we are reminded of this when, after the Our Father, the celebrant prays the words "we await the blessed hope and the coming of our Savior, Jesus Christ." Our "waiting" is filled with joy, because when Christ returns, our salvation is fulfilled and all evil is conquered. Our waiting is filled with hope, because Christ embodies all we long for. Our waiting is active, not passive, because the fruits of our efforts at building a world of justice, love and peace will not be lost when Christ returns. Rather, "we will find them once again, cleansed this time from stain of sin, illuminated and transfigured" (Second Vatican Council, *Gaudium et Spes,* n.39).

A key way to celebrate Advent, therefore, is to focus on how our daily activity can increase these fruits of justice and peace in the world. The Lord wants to find us active upon his return, active in establishing the Kingdom which he comes to fulfill. The work of defending human life is central to that Kingdom. Advent is a perfect time to rededicate ourselves to proclaim, celebrate and serve the Gospel of Life. It is a perfect time for parishes to start or strengthen respect life committees, or to have public commissioning of such groups.

Lord, at your coming, may you find us already welcoming you in our daily welcome of the most vulnerable brothers and sisters!

# ADVENT: A SUMMONS TO REPENTANCE

In "Advent," which means "coming," we focus on the coming of Christ at the end of time, and then on his first coming at Christmas. Advent is marked by the joy of his coming, but also by the strong warning that we must be prepared for it, as individuals and as a community.

Hence, a key theme of Advent is repentance.

John the Baptizer prepared the people for the coming of Christ by proclaiming repentance, so the Church prepares the world for his second coming by likewise proclaiming, and opening the way, for repentance.

The third chapter of Matthew's Gospel begins, *"In those days John the Baptist came, preaching in the Desert of Judea and saying, 'Repent, for the kingdom of heaven is near.' This is he who was spoken of through the prophet Isaiah: A voice of one calling in the desert, 'Prepare the way for the Lord, make straight paths for him.'"*

He says, furthermore, continuing the quote from Isaiah, "*Every valley shall be filled in, every mountain and hill made low. The crooked roads shall become straight, the rough ways smooth*" (Luke 3:5).

Christ's coming ushers in the final triumph of life over death. The preparation for that coming, therefore, includes repentance from the works of death, including abortion. Not only individuals but nations likewise need to repent. This repentance includes living with active respect for every human life, and building a society of justice and welcome for the most vulnerable.

"Prepare the way of the Lord," who is a God of Justice. "Every valley shall be filled" – the valleys where people languish because their rights are trampled, their dignity forgotten, and their lives thrown onto the outskirts of society. "Every mountain and hill shall be made low" – the mountains of pride whereby we think our own choices determine what is right and wrong, rather than submitting our choices to the truth that became visible when Christ was born.

Promoting justice and human rights is a key element of our preparation. A society that aborts its children is not prepared for the coming of Christ. Individuals who ignore the massive slaughter of tens of millions of babies are not prepared to welcome the God who became a little baby.

Nor are they prepared to welcome the gifts the baby brings. To welcome Christ is to welcome the one who teaches the Gospels, establishes his Church, and brings us the Eucharist and the other sacraments. Some want to welcome Christ only by welcoming the baby, but not staying around long enough to hear what he has to say or receive what he comes to bring.

Advent repentance means we are to open our Christmas gifts: Accept the teachings of the Church which the newborn child founded as an adult, utilize the sacrament of penance to receive his forgiveness, accept the grace that enables us to repent of sin, receive him in the Eucharist faithfully, and let him work through us to build a society of justice and a Culture of Life.

# Advent: A Summons to Courage

Advent focuses our minds and hearts on the Second Coming of Christ. At a time nobody knows, he will return to earth, separate good from evil entirely, and publicly judge every person who ever lived. All the good we have done, especially at the price of ridicule, will be rewarded in the presence of the entire human family and the saints of all time. Those who ridiculed us, especially for our pro-life stance, will be proven wrong, and will be ashamed of not having stood for life.

As Advent reminds us of these things, it strengthens us to be even bolder in speaking up for what is true and right. In the light of the eternal judgment and the Second Coming of Christ, what sacrifice is too great to make for our smallest brothers and sisters who need our help today?

When we battle against the Culture of Death in its various forms, we may often pray, "Lord, rend the heavens and come down!" Why, for example, does the Lord just not appear from the sky to stop the abortions from happening?

The fact is that he *did* come down in the Incarnation of Jesus Christ, and through the Lord's clear teachings continues to put the truth in our minds, and the grace in our hearts, so that we can be the ones who bear witness to life amid the Culture of Death, work tirelessly to transform that culture, and intervene to save the helpless.

In the light of the fact that he has come and will come again, let us carry out that task with unwavering courage!

# Advent Reconciles Mother and Preborn Child

The introduction to the lectionary, when speaking of the Sundays of Advent, says, "Each Gospel reading has a specific theme: The Lord's coming in glory at the end of time (first Sunday), John the Baptist (second and third Sundays), and the events which immediately prepared for the Lord's birth (fourth Sunday)" (No.11).

We focus, in other words, on the first and second comings of the same Christ, and on the one who teaches us how to prepare for his arrival, namely, by repentance. "Reform your lives! The reign of God is at hand." The New Testament readings throughout Advent complement and expand on John the Baptist's exhortations of repentance.

The preparation for Christ's coming is reform, and the promise of his coming is reconciliation. The two, furthermore, are linked. If the Messiah comes to restore harmony between nations and people, then the people of the Messiah are to repent of whatever destroys that harmony. If the Messiah comes to bring justice ("He shall judge the poor with justice and decide aright for the land's afflicted"), then the people of the Messiah are to work to eliminate injustice. The "justice" referred to in Isaiah 11 is an act of intervention to save the helpless.

Abortion is an injustice against the most helpless, and attacks the harmony of human relationships at their most fundamental and sensitive point, the relationship of mother and child. Preparing for the Lord's coming therefore requires a total rejection of abortion. The promise of his coming heralds a new harmony between mother and child.

The focus on the Virgin and Child at the end of Advent highlights this.

The Second Vatican Council reflects upon the relationship between the coming of Christ and our activity to prepare for it. In the Constitution on the Church in the Modern World, we read, *"Far from diminishing our concern to develop this earth, the expectancy of a new earth should spur us on, for it is here that the body of a new human family grows, foreshadowing in some way the age which is to come.... When we have spread on earth the fruits of our nature and our enterprise -- human dignity, brotherly communion and freedom -- according to the command of the Lord and in his Spirit, we will find them once again, cleansed this time from the stain of sin, illuminated and transfigured, when Christ presents to his Father an eternal and universal kingdom...."* (#39). In other words, the spirit of Advent should naturally bolster our pro-life efforts, and the progress we make in promoting human dignity becomes the "building blocks" for the eternal kingdom.

Advent leads the Church to the Silent Night when God Himself is revealed as one of us. This season leads us to the joy of his birth. May that birth shed protection on all about to be born, and as we work to end abortion, may we, as the liturgy says, "await the blessed hope and the coming of Our Savior, Jesus Christ."

# O COME, O COME, EMANUEL!

"O Come, O Come, Emanuel, and ransom captive Israel..."

It is perhaps the most well-known Advent hymn, one which begins to flood us with the feelings of the coming Christmas season.

But the hymn raises a question. Matthew's Gospel tells us that "Emanuel" means "God is with us" (Mt. 1:23). So in the song we pray, "O come, O come, God who is already with us!" If he is with us, why are we asking him to come?

The reason is that when he comes, he changes and transforms us, and because we are free to thwart and slow down that process of change, there is always more changing that we need. God indeed loves us as we are, but he loves us too much to let us remain the way we are. There is more of God that we can receive, more about him that we can know, more of our old ways that we can cast off, more of the grace of Christ that we can live by. He wants to come to every corner of our world, and transform every aspect of our lives. Though we have received him before, there are dark corners to which we have not yet invited him. "O come, O come, God who is with us, come to the places where we have not yet allowed you to transform us. Come and remove the sin we still cling to; come and give us the compassion and virtue we do not yet have!"

There is always more of God to receive. To have received him all, one would have to *be* God. He comes in manifold ways: Through created reality and relationships, through prayer, through suffering, through acts of charity, through Scripture, through the ministers of the Church, through the fellowship of believers, and through the Sacraments. He will come again in glory, on a day we do not know, at the culmination of human history.

We ask him to come and "ransom captive Israel." He ransoms us personally, and he ransoms us as a society. Praying for his coming, therefore, does not mean simply waiting and looking forward to it. It means preparing for it, and casting aside the obstacles in the way.

One key way that our society needs to prepare for the coming of the one who saves us is to work steadfastly to save one another, and to remove all oppression of the human person. A glaring need here is to restore protection to unborn children. To claim the right to permit the killing of children by abortion is to cease to acknowledge the dominion of the one who comes. It is to refuse to make room for the justice he comes to bring.

The beautiful hymn "O Holy Night" sums it up in the verse that says, *"Truly he taught us to love one another; his law is love and his gospel is peace. Chains shall he break, for the slave is our brother, and in his name all oppression shall cease!"*

# RUSHING TO THE SIDE OF MARY

In the second half of Advent the liturgy focuses more specifically on the incarnation and birth of Jesus at the first Christmas.

We think about Mary's initial fear and uncertainty in the face of her unexpected pregnancy. When the Archangel Gabriel announced to her that she would conceive and bear a son, Scripture tells us, *"Mary was greatly troubled at his words and wondered what kind of greeting this might be"* (Luke 1:29). Once told of the message, she expressed her doubt and confusion: *"'How will this be,' Mary asked the angel, 'since I am a virgin?'"* (Luke 1:34).

Of course, the Archangel reassures her with the oft-repeated biblical words, "Be not afraid," explaining that everything will take place through the power and providence of God, who has a clear plan that -- with her cooperation -- will unfold for the good of the whole world.

Mary is consoled, though still not understanding the whole picture, and is led to express her trust and consent to God's will: *"Fiat - Be it done unto me according to your word" (Luke 1:38).* It is, in fact, at the moment of this "Yes" that the Son of God is conceived within Mary's body. Her "Yes" leads to life.

As the members of the Church hear this story again in Advent, they rush spiritually to the side of Mary in grateful wonder and with the support appropriate to sons and daughters. They eagerly await with her the birth of the Savior.

The best way for a parish to celebrate Advent and Christmas, then, is to rush physically to the side of those in the community who, like Mary, are uncertain and afraid about their pregnancy. We are to accompany them through their pregnancy with support and encouragement, help them to say the "Yes" that leads to life, and experience with them the fact that every birth reflects the joy of the birth of Christ.

This is possible when the Church raises awareness that there are alternatives to abortion, and that there are many people ready to provide those alternatives. Through the preaching and teaching that the Church carries out among its own members, and through announcing this message to the wider community, the Church saves lives and enables parents to live their calling.

This can be done by cooperation with the many pregnancy resource centers which, across the nation, are daily providing counseling, encouragement, medical and legal services, and other material and spiritual assistance, to those who otherwise might have an abortion. Churches should publicize the "Option Line" which is a toll-free number (1-800-712-HELP) and a website (***www.PregnancyCenters.org***) that leads people to the pregnancy centers nearest to where they live. Likewise, www.PregnancyDecisionLine.org is an online resource Churches can promote to help women who are abortion minded to find the counseling needed to change their mind.

Churches also need to mobilize their own resources, calling upon medical and legal professionals within the congregation, as well as parishioners who may want to give of their time to be a friend to pregnant mothers or open their homes to give them a place to stay. In this way the Church can become the place of "first resort" for someone who is pregnant and afraid. It should be the Church, not the abortion mill, to which she first comes to knock on the door. The Gabriel Project, now operating in various dioceses, is a model for this kind of initiative.

To promote awareness and assistance, furthermore, many parishes have "Baby Showers" and "Spiritual Adoption Programs" of various formats, whereby the parishioners follow the development of a baby in the womb for nine months and then, at the conclusion, gather resources to give to local pregnancy centers to help mothers and fathers in need.

The birth of every child reflects the birth of Christ. Let there be joy in both. Let Advent and Christmas inspire us to rush to the side of all pregnant moms and say, "Be not afraid!"

# Born of a Virgin

On the verge of Christmas, on the verge of the celebration of welcoming Christ into the world, the Church's liturgy focuses on the virginity of Mary. In conceiving and giving birth to Christ, Mary did not lose that virginity, nor did she lose it at any time later in her life.

Both in the Old and New Testaments, virginity has a powerful symbolic message about the relationship of God to his people. God wants to marry his people. Their fidelity to him, and their rejection of idols and false gods, is symbolized by virginity.

Mary symbolizes the whole Church. She received Christ into her virginal body. The Church, too, as the Bride of Christ – and each of us individually – is called to a total fidelity that is symbolized by the virginity of Mary.

In other words, whatever the vocation of each of us, this spiritual (if not physical) virginity means we have no Lord besides Jesus. We do not worship false gods or become intimate with other deities.

As Mary welcomed Christ in her virginity, so does the Church. "It is through the Holy Spirit that this child has been conceived in her," the Gospel tells us. So can we say, "It is through the Holy Spirit that this child has been conceived in us," and "It is through the Holy Spirit that this child has been conceived in the world." No human effort brings about Christmas. But by our "virginal" fidelity, the Spirit brings him forth into the world through us.

This is the "obedience of faith" of which St. Paul speaks.

And part of this virginal fidelity, part of this obedience of faith, is our commitment to be pro-life. "God is with us" means that he is on the side of every human life, against all that would destroy it. So must we be.

# St. Juan Diego and Our Lady of Guadalupe

During the Advent season, the Church also celebrates the feast of Our Lady of Guadalupe (December 12) and that of Saint Juan Diego (December 9), to whom she appeared. The timing of these feasts within Advent is appropriate, since they are related to the Advent-Christmas themes, as well as to the unborn.

At the time Our Lady of Guadalupe appeared to Juan Diego in 1531 in Mexico, the Aztec peoples were practicing human sacrifice. As a result of the image's presence among the people, their hearts were converted to the true God and the practice of human sacrifice was abolished. A key theological dynamic operating here is that Our Lady turned the Aztecs from a worldview of despair to one of hope, from a conviction that the gods were against them to a conviction that God was so much *for* them that *he became one of them.*

The Aztecs had a complicated mythology-theology. The universe for them was essentially unstable, and in that universe humans played a very small role. This view led to pessimism, and a fear that they needed to always appease the deities. Their view was that the present world was the "Fifth world," made by the "Feathered Serpent." The previous four worlds had been destroyed by gods who turned people into monkeys or dogs. The present world, they thought, would be destroyed by an earthquake, as a result of which skeleton creatures would come out of the ground to destroy the surviving inhabitants of earth.

This is a theology of despair. Whatever moral aversion they may have had to human sacrifice, their despair made them feel they had no choice but to practice it.

How does the image of Our Lady of Guadalupe answer the theology of despair, both for the Aztecs and for the Americas?

Our Lady is carrying *God* within her womb. The God of the Universe has now *become* a human being. No longer is there any question as to whether God is on our side. He is not a God who will destroy us; He is a God who has become our brother. He is not a God far away who waits to be appeased by blood. He is a God who shares our own flesh and blood, and is as close to the human family as an unborn child to his mother.

In this framework, human beings no longer play a *small part* in the universe. On the contrary, as the Second Vatican Council proclaimed, "By his incarnation the Son of God has united himself in some fashion with every human being" (Pastoral Constitution on the Church in the Modern World *Gaudium et Spes*, 22). The result of that is the promise of Revelation 3:21, "I will give the victor the right to sit with me on my throne."

The universe into which Our Lady of Guadalupe invites

us is no longer an unstable universe. God clearly reveals himself as the only God, who *is* and *shares* both love and life. This truth brings *hope.* There is no longer need for human sacrifice, whether on pagan altars or in abortion clinics, because both the present and the future are in the hands of a God who is "God with us."

Abortion is a sin against both life and hope. Those who abort their children do not do so out of choice, but out of despair. As author Frederica Mathewes-Green has said, a woman does not choose an abortion like she chooses a Porsche or an ice-cream -- rather, she chooses it like an animal caught in a trap chooses to gnaw off its own leg.

But the God in the womb, and his mother who says "Yes," give new courage and hope. God continues to reveal himself in the tiny babies yet in the womb. He invites us to see him in them, and to love him in them! Christmas gives us the strength to say "Yes" to life!

# CHRISTMAS: FEAST OF THE INCARNATION

Christmas is not simply the feast of the birth of Christ; it is the feast of his *becoming human,* the reality called the *Incarnation* (In Latin, the words "*in carne*" mean "*in flesh*"). Christ, who existed from all eternity as God, took flesh within the body of the Virgin Mary when she said "Yes" to his coming, nine months before his birth.

Christmas, in its full meaning, is the feast that celebrates that moment, along with his birth, as one wonderful reality of God becoming one of us. Christmas, in other words, is more than the feast of the *birth* of Christ. Historically, the Christmas traditions have come to focus mostly on his actual birth which, of course, deserves all the celebration with which we honor it.

But Christmas, originally and fundamentally, is the feast of the *Incarnation.*

We can best understand "Incarnation" by thinking for a moment about Jesus' title "Son of God." When a parent has a son in a human family, it is clear that there was a time when the parent existed but the son did not. The parent has more experience, wisdom, and strength than the son.

But this is not the case with Jesus.

There was never a time that the Father existed but the Son did not. He always was. Furthermore, all the wisdom and power of the Father belong also to the Son. The Son is "God from God, Light from Light, True God from True God, *begotten, not made, consubstantial with the Father*" (Creed). Simply put, the Son of God *is* God.

Christmas, then, is not when Jesus began existing. Christmas, and hence the Incarnation, is about Jesus beginning to exist as a human being. (This begins to happen, of course, nine months before his birth.) The Divine Person shared our human nature. One of our brothers in the human family is God.

When God makes people, he creates a human body and soul and says, "This is yours!" In the Incarnation, he creates a human body and soul, and says, "This is *mine!*"

The Second Vatican Council drew out a key implication of this doctrine: *"By his incarnation the Son of God has united himself in some fashion with every human being"* (Pastoral Constitution on the Church in the Modern World, *Gaudium et Spes*, 22). Without denying the doctrine of the necessity of evangelization and baptism, this truth is a profound basis for our seeing every human being as a brother or sister. This doctrinal truth is in turn the source of the moral obligation to care for each other.

Human life was already sacred because it always was

and is God's creation, made freely from his love. But in the Incarnation it takes on an even deeper meaning and sanctity, because human nature is forever united with Divine Life. This affects all who share human nature, even the children still in the womb.

In this context, *The Gospel of Life* states, "*It is precisely in the 'flesh' of every person that Christ continues to reveal himself and to enter into fellowship with us, so that rejection of human life, in whatever form that rejection takes, is really a rejection of Christ" (EV #104).*

Likewise, in another passage, the encyclical states,

"Life, especially human life, belongs only to God: for this reason *whoever attacks human life, in some way attacks God himself*" (EV n. 9).

There are two days in the Church's liturgical year in which the rubrics of the Mass indicate that the people need to genuflect during the Creed, specifically at the mention of God taking on flesh. Those days are the Solemnity of the Annunciation (March 25) and Christmas Day. At the Annunciation, the Incarnation occurred and Jesus became an unborn child at Mary's "Yes." Nine months later, he was born. Both feasts celebrate the same wonder of the Incarnation, with different historical emphases.

The Fathers of the Church commented that what Jesus redeemed, he "assumed," that is, took upon himself. He took on our human nature to redeem it. And he took on life in the womb. God was a zygote, an embryo, a fetus, an unborn child. He united to himself, in Christ, every zygote, embryo, and fetus -- in other words, every human life at every stage of development. Human life, which was already sacred because it comes from God, was hence made even more holy, and worthy of our every sacrifice.

This truth has led to various devotions and writings in honor of "The Unborn Jesus," "The Redeemer in the Womb." Contemplating Jesus at that stage of his existence, and indeed worshipping him as an unborn child, is an appropriate stimulus to our pro-life commitment.

Pope Benedict XVI, wishing to reinforce this truth for the whole world, opened the Season of Advent on November 27, 2010 with a prayer vigil in St. Peter's Basilica at the Vatican for the intention of all human life yet in the womb. He asked dioceses throughout the world to take part in this Vigil for Life, and preached about how Advent shows us the sanctity of life at all stages.

The meaning of Christmas is completely incompatible with any acceptance of abortion. May this Christmas reinforce that truth in our hearts and our entire world.

# GOD IN HUMAN LANGUAGE

Christmas is *God in human language.*

It is about a God who, in love with us from eternity and having made us out of nothing, knows how to speak to us.

As the Letter to the Hebrews tells us, "*In the past God spoke to our forefathers through the prophets at many times and in various ways, but in these last days he has spoken to us by his Son*" (Heb. 1:1-2).

Christmas is *revelation, manifestation, showing what was hidden.* When the Advent prayers cry out, "Open up, ye heavens from above!" one of the sentiments being expressed is the human need for *meaning,* and for the answers to basic questions: *Why are we here? What is this life about? Where are we going? Is there life after death? How are we supposed to live? Does God exist, and if so, what does he think of me? Is he friend or foe? How does he want to be worshipped?*

All the philosophers of all the ages, though coming to certain conclusions correctly because of the power of human reason (which, though wounded by sin, is not destroyed) nevertheless could not reach the fullness of the answers to all these questions. *God needed to speak, and he needed to speak in human language.*

So the Son who is the revelation of the Father has come,

and Christmas celebrates that coming. Continuing that passage from Hebrews, which, incidentally, is one of the readings used by the Church for Christmas Day Mass, we read, "*The Son is the radiance of God's glory and the exact representation of his being*" (v. 3).

So, thanks to Christmas, we know who God is, what life is about, what God expects us to do, and what awaits us beyond the grave. We know how to obtain eternal life. We have found what the human heart has longed for forever. St. John writes, "*After this I looked, and there before me was a door standing open in heaven*" (Revelation 4:1). Christmas opens that door and shows us God in human language, bringing us certainty in the truths of our faith.

Christmas, in other words, destroys the "tyranny of relativism," the confusion of indifferentism, the idea that each person can create his or her own morality, the idea that one religion is as good as the next. As we welcome the birth of this child, we welcome the one who will preach the Sermon on the Mount, instruct us by parables, and establish his Church to continue making his teachings clear.

To welcome the Divine Child today is to welcome all that he will do and teach, the easy and the difficult, the comforting and the challenging, without considering ourselves authorized to edit, delete, or pick and choose among those teachings.

It makes no sense to welcome the child but reject his teachings. It is inconsistent to prepare for and celebrate

Christmas but refuse to accept the fullness of the Gospel that this child proclaimed.

That Gospel has taught from the beginning that life must be protected, including life in the womb. There can be no such thing as a “pro-choice Christian.” A rejection of even a single life is a rejection of Christ himself.

This Advent and Christmas, let us welcome Christ and all that he teaches, and all whom he loves.

# WHAT THE SHEPHERDS UNDERSTOOD

One translation of Luke 2:17 tells us that on the first Christmas, when the shepherds arrived in Bethlehem and saw the baby in the manger, they ***understood*** what had been told to them by the angels who appeared to them in the middle of the night to announce the birth of Christ.

Why was it at the moment they arrived at the manger that they understood the message?

Perhaps it is because a baby is so approachable. After all, the angels said that the Savior was born for *all people.* Nobody, no matter how poor or lowly, should be afraid to approach him. And how can God become more approachable than by becoming a little baby?

Many people believe in God, but are scared of him. Who is he, they wonder, does he like me, and is he on my side? Seeing God as a baby answers all these questions and reassures us beyond words.

Christmas is about "God and sinners reconciled." It is the manifestation of how "God so loved the world" (John 3:16) that he gave his Son to save us. In doing this, the Son of God did not *leave* heaven, because as God, he is always there. But what is conveyed by the language of "leaving" or "coming down" from heaven is that he shows himself to us in a more approachable form. He leaves behind, for a little while, the blazing and terrifying glory, the thunder and lightning, and the kingly appearance about which we read in so many of the manifestations of God (see, for instance, Exodus 19:16 as it relates God's presence on Mount Sinai).

God "came down" from that form and made himself a baby. This would help the Shepherds understand that, indeed, this Savior was for everyone, including the most humble and lowly, including those who were afraid of any appearance of God, and including those who think that God is only out to get them, to punish them or to destroy them.

The fact that God becomes a baby means that we can drop all fear; it means he will even become vulnerable for us, so that we can really get to know him and be close to him. That is why he is for *all people,* and that is why, indeed, his birth is a cause for *great joy.*

# CHRISTMAS: WERE YOU THERE?

On Good Friday, we sing, "Were You There When They Crucified My Lord?" It makes us think of what it would have been like to see Jesus on the cross, and to stand along with Mary, St. John, and the others on the first Good Friday. It is, indeed, one of the most moving of Christian hymns, particularly because the answer to the question is "Yes." We *were* there, because He died for us, and our sins were on His shoulders. We *are* there, as He renews that very sacrifice on our altars each day at Mass, and we freely unite our own sacrifices with His.

What about Christmas? What if we sang, "Were you there when the King of Kings was born?" Nativity scenes, and the meditations which spiritual writers provide us about that first Christmas, help us enter in to the drama and meaning of that event.

St. Pope John Paul II indicated to us that there is indeed a way to *be there* at the first Christmas, too. He wrote the following in his encyclical *The Gospel of Life:*

*"At the dawn of salvation, it is the Birth of a Child which is proclaimed as joyful news: 'I bring you good news of a great joy which will come to all the people; for to you is born this day in the city of David a Savior, who is Christ the Lord' (Lk 2:10-11). The source of this 'great joy' is the Birth of the Savior; but Christmas also reveals the full meaning of every human birth, and the joy which accompanies the Birth of the Messiah is thus*

*seen to be the foundation and fulfillment of joy at every child born into the world (cf. Jn 16:21)" (EV, 1).*

St. John Paul linked the birth of Jesus Christ with the birth of every child, and he did so on the level of *meaning* and *joy*.

"Christmas … reveals the full meaning of every human birth." Christmas is God joining himself to us, giving himself to us -- in fact, *marrying us*. That also is why each human person comes into the world. The meaning of life is to give and receive love; to give ourselves to God and one another; to achieve the union with God -- in this life and the next -- which is the very purpose of our existence.

The joy of Jesus' birth is "the foundation and fulfillment of joy at every child born into the world." God did not have to come to us, nor did he have to create us. But in fact he does both. Each life, like Christmas itself, is a sign of God's love, a sign that God has not given up on the world, a sign that he keeps giving us a chance. Each life, no matter how limited, is a reflection of the glory of God.

*The Gospel of Life* also tells us,

> "*Why is life a good?* This question is found everywhere in the Bible, and from the very first pages it receives a powerful and amazing answer. The life which God gives man is quite different from the life of all other living

> creatures, inasmuch as man, although formed from the dust of the earth (cf. *Gen* 2:7, 3:19; *Job* 34:15; *Ps* 103:14; 104:29), *is a manifestation of God in the world, a sign of his presence, a trace of his glory* (cf. *Gen* 1:26-27; *Ps* 8:6). This is what Saint Irenaeus of Lyons wanted to emphasize in his celebrated definition: 'Man, living man, is the glory of God.' Man has been given *a sublime dignity,* based on the intimate bond which unites him to his Creator: in man there shines forth a reflection of God himself *(EV, 34).*

So, yes, we were there at Christmas. We are there, each time we draw near, in loving compassion and service, to any human life, born or unborn, drawn to that life because we are aware that it is a reflection of the glory of God himself. As the Word made Flesh is the *perfect* and *exact* representation of the Father's glory, so each human being is a reflection of that same glory.

Let us, then, celebrate Christmas by recommitting ourselves to being truly pro-life!

# CHRISTMAS: SEASON OF LIFE

St. Augustine said of Christmas, "God became man so that man might become God."

Christmas is about a wondrous exchange of natures: God takes on himself our frail humanity, though without its sin, and we become partakers of the very nature of God (see 2 Peter 1:4). The joy of Christmas is not just that a child is born, but that a whole new humanity is born. This new humanity is not disconnected from the old, but is radically renewed and redeemed. Just as in Adam, all die, so in Christ shall all be made alive (see Romans 5:12-19).

Christmas, then, is about the destiny of the human person. In the Book of Revelation, we read this promise of the Risen Christ to his faithful disciples: "I will give the victor the right to sit with me on my throne" (Rev. 3:21). Thrones, at the time of the New Testament, characteristically allowed more than one person to sit on them. In heaven, we will not only *see* God's throne, or gather *around* God's throne; rather, you and I have a place *on* the very throne of God!

Now some want to give Christmas a totally "this-worldly" meaning: Kindness, goodness, the importance of family, joy, and giving. These are all natural values and have meaning for the Christian. But the Christmas message goes far beyond these good things, and talks about where we are ultimately going, and what kind of destiny awaits us beyond the grave. Moreover, the Faith teaches that this destiny *begins even now.* "He who believes *has* eternal life" (John 6:47).

Christmas, then, is about the Gospel of Life. It is about the hope of eternal life offered through the birth of a child, and through our birth into his life by our faith. Christmas, then, illumines the meaning and value of every human person. In the light of the manger, we see every human person as one who is called to share the Divine Nature, as one called to *sit with Christ on his throne!*

Is it possible for one to accept the Christmas message, and then to turn the other way when human life is despised and destroyed? Can the Christian, who declares that the human person is called to the very heights of heaven, stand idly by when those same human beings are thrown in the garbage by abortion, or disposed of by euthanasia?

The hymn "O Holy Night" sums up this lesson in the verse "Truly He taught us to love one another; His law is love, and his Gospel is peace. Chains shall he break, for the slave is our brother, and in his name, all oppression shall cease."

That's how I celebrate Christmas each year: A complete rededication to ending abortion, the worst form of oppression of my brothers and sisters. I hope that's how you celebrate it, too. A child is born, and his birth immerses us in the defense and celebration of *life!*

# CHOICE ON EARTH

Christmas cards come in many shapes, sizes, and themes. Even the nation's largest abortion business, Planned Parenthood, has offered its own take on a Christmas card.

The message of the card unveiled several years ago?

"Choice on Earth."

Planned Parenthood advertised the card as containing "an inclusive seasonal message." Inclusive for everyone, of course, except the unborn child, who is destroyed by the so-called "choice" that Planned Parenthood promotes.

But, of course, Planned Parenthood was not ashamed. In fact, when the card was called anti-Christian, they responded by adding a "Choice on Earth" T-shirt to their line of products.

Added to this, some who call themselves ministers of the Gospel preached their seasonal message by claiming that Jesus would not have been against the "choice" of a woman regarding whether or not to continue her pregnancy. You may be aware that there is a "Clergy for Choice Network" operated by the "Religious Coalition for Reproductive Choice."

My comment on all of this is that it should not surprise us in the least. The essence of the abortion mentality is *not* to deny that the unborn child is a child. Rather, it is that *we take the place of God.* It is the idea that *what I choose is right*, not because the thing I choose is *good*, but rather because *I choose.* Choice is more important than life, and my choice takes the place of God Himself. Hence, clergy preach "choice" and the message of Christ becomes "Choice on Earth."

Ultimately, human beings have to feel like they are in line with God. Therefore, if they do not change their lives to conform to God's will, they will change their very concept of God to conform to their own will. That's what the "Choice on Earth" cards demonstrated.

The notion that Christ does not have a problem with the choice to destroy an unborn child turns the Gospel inside out. By giving His life for us, Christ teaches the essence of love: *I sacrifice myself for the good of the other person.* Abortion teaches exactly the opposite message: *I sacrifice the other person for the good of myself.*

Jesus, furthermore, broke down false barriers that placed people in "higher" and "lower" social and spiritual categories. He ate with tax collectors and sinners when the common wisdom was to avoid them. He sought out the lepers when the custom was to stay away from them. He called the children to come to him, when the apostles thought the right thing to do was to chase them away. He gave the Samaritan woman the gift of salvation, breaking through barriers that put both Samaritans and women on a lower level.

Does it make sense, then, that the Lord permits the false barrier between the born and the unborn, and does not mind the discrimination by which the unborn are considered disposable *non-persons?*

God is a God of *justice* -- in other words, He saves the helpless. And he expects us to do no less. *That's* peace on earth.

# GROWN-UP CHRISTMAS LIST

One of the songs you'll hear on the radio during the Christmas season is called "*Grown-up Christmas List*." It speaks of the fact that age does not stop us from dreaming, and that as life goes on, our wishes at Christmas are not for ourselves, "but for a world in need." The list begins, *"No more lives torn apart, that wars would never start…that right would always win."*

Do we dare to hope for these things, just because the calendar says December 25 is approaching?

Indeed, the question for a Christian is, "How we can dare *not to hope for these things?"* Christmas lists, after all, spring from Christmas hope, and Christmas hope is based on an historical fact: *God has already given us everything in his son.* St. Paul asks, "He who did not spare his own son, but gave him up for us all—how will he not also, along with him, graciously give us all things?" (Rom. 8:32).

We look for good things in life, and good things are all around us. Yet the best of good things does not satisfy us completely. The best relationships leave something to be desired, and the best vacations always end and leave us looking forward to the next one. This is because every good thing is just a reflection of *goodness itself.*

In the birth of Christ, we find that total, infinite

goodness. *"For in Christ all the fullness of the Deity lives in bodily form" (Col. 2:9). "The son is the radiance of God's glory and the exact representation of his being" (Heb. 1:3).* In the birth of Jesus Christ, almighty God has given to the human family his last, best offer of hope.

The wonder of Christmas, in fact, is that the promised coming of the Messiah *of the Lord* was fulfilled in a surprising way that surpassed the hopes and dreams of the people of old. From the beginning of time, prophets announced that the *Messiah of the Lord* would come. "Messiah," or "Christ" means "Anointed one." God anointed many people to carry out special missions for him. The Anointed Messiah, then, would have the most special mission of all, to bring about the definitive kingdom of God.

On the first Christmas night, angels announced Christ's birth to the shepherds. But instead of saying that Jesus was the Messiah *of the Lord,* they said he is "Messiah *and Lord*" (Lk. 2:11). God, in other words, did not simply send someone to represent him. *He came himself!*

Christmas is not about the birth of a child who became a great man. It is about a God who created the human family, and then decided to become a member of that family. Christmas is not when Jesus began; it is when Jesus began existing as one of us, *and thereby joined all of us to himself.* He joins to his divinity all who share human nature: The weak and strong, the small and big, the born and unborn. *Christmas is universal, and is about the exaltation of the human person.*

That's why our "grown-up Christmas list" can say "no more lives torn apart" -- whether by abortion or anything else.

The song goes on, "*As children we believed the grandest sight to see was something lovely wrapped beneath the tree. But heaven only knows that packages and bows can never heal a hurting human soul.*"

To see the grandest sight, one that can indeed heal our soul, is to behold the God who became one of us in Christ.

Christmas lists spring from Christmas hope, and Christmas is all about *the victory of life*!

Fr. Frank Pavone

# CHRISTMAS, CHRISTIANS, AND CHRIST

Some years ago, a class of students was asked to write about the meaning of Christmas. One student wrote, "Christmas is when Christians celebrate Christ." The teacher liked the paper, but asked the student to change that one line to "Christmas is when people celebrate love."

What, some may wonder, is the difference? After all, Christians are people and Christ is love.

Yet there is a difference – and the difference is so profound that if we miss it, we have missed the meaning of Christmas and Christ.

Of course, Christians are people. But not all people are Christians. To be a Christian is much more than to be a good person. It's about becoming a *new* person, sharing a *new kind of life – the life of God himself.* Christmas is not just about the birth of a child; it's about the birth of a whole new humanity. In Adam, all die; in Christ, all come to life again. We are made sharers, by faith and baptism, in the Divine Nature. At every Mass, as he pours a few drops of water into the wine, the priest prays, "By the mystery of this water and wine, may we come to share in the Divinity of Christ, who humbled himself to share in our humanity."

That's what Christmas is all about. St. Augustine put

it this way: "God became man that man might become God." In the Book of Revelation, the Risen Christ tells his faithful disciples: "I will give the victor the right to sit with me on my throne" (Rev. 3:21).

Preaching today too often loses sight of this fundamental dimension of the Gospel. And people therefore risk seeing Christmas as being just about good cheer, giving, family, and peace on earth. It is about those things, but only because it is first about God reconciling humanity to himself in Christ and opening the way for humanity to share divine life. Christmas is a *Christian* feast.

And then there's the meaning of "love." Yes, people celebrate love at Christmas, but it is only *in Christ* that we fully learn the nature of love and find the power to practice it. "Love one another as I have loved you," he commanded us. The love we are called to live is a love that is revealed in the Christ who gives himself on the cross, and a love that requires us to give our lives for one another. It is a love shaped by the first and greatest commandment: Love the Lord your God with all your heart, mind, soul, and strength. Without the love of God, we cannot find the strength to love one another. And without Christ, we do not see the full revelation of God.

Love has a content, and that content is defined by the Gospel of Jesus Christ. Love is not simply the good intention, or the context, in which we do whatever we think is best. Love always requires certain actions and always prohibits certain actions.

At Christmas, God calls all people to celebrate the love that took flesh in Christ, by believing in him and following him in the new, eternal life he brings.

# DR. KING'S CHRISTMAS SERMON

On Christmas 1967, the Rev. Dr. Martin Luther King Jr. preached the following words: *"The next thing we must be concerned about if we are to have peace on earth and good will toward men is the nonviolent affirmation of the sacredness of all human life. Every man is somebody because he is a child of God...Man is more than ...whirling electrons or a wisp of smoke .... Man is a child of God, made in His image, and therefore must be respected as such....And when we truly believe in the sacredness of human personality, we won't exploit people, we won't trample over people with the iron feet of oppression, we won't kill anybody.*"

Christmas is a marvelous celebration. I love the festivity and decorations, the music and the meals. Christmas celebrates the greatest gift that we receive, Jesus Christ, and should therefore be a season of great festivity.

But in receiving such a tremendous gift, we receive a correspondingly great obligation, namely, the *duty to welcome.* Christ comes, but he does not come alone. He brings his love, but in doing so, he brings us the burden of loving all whom he loves.

Christ comes to reconcile us to the Father and to one another. He does this in an unspeakably profound way: *He makes us his Body.* St. Paul teaches it clearly: "*Do you not know that your bodies are members of Christ himself?"* (1 Cor. 6:15). *"In Christ we who are many form one body, and each member belongs to all the others"* (Rom. 12:5).

All human beings share the nature Christ took upon himself, and every human being is called to be part of the Body. Christ excludes nobody from his love, and so neither can we.

Christmas, therefore, takes away the option of excluding people from our love. God has a face now, and in that face we understand the dignity of all who share human nature, including our brothers and sisters in the womb. They, of course, are the easiest to exclude. In her famous song "We are One Body," the singer Dana Skovall includes the words, "*See the unborn baby, the forgotten one, they are not forsaken, they are not unloved.*"

We also understand that all who share that human nature belong to the one who takes that nature upon himself at Christmas. This Feast makes it clear that no human being can own another, or oppress another. Now, one of our brothers in the human family is *God.* To claim to be able to own or oppress anyone who shares a human nature is, therefore, to claim to be able to own and oppress God himself.

Vatican II taught, "*By his incarnation the Son of God has united himself in some fashion with every human being*" (*GS,* 22). Hence *The Gospel of Life* states, "*It is precisely in the 'flesh' of every person that Christ continues to reveal himself and to enter into fellowship with us, so that rejection of human life, in whatever form that rejection takes, is really a rejection of Christ" (EV #104)* and again, *"life, especially human life, belongs only to God: for this reason whoever attacks human life, in some way attacks God himself" (EV #9).*

Christmas is about welcome; abortion is about rejection. St. Paul writes, "Welcome one another as Christ welcomed you," (Rom. 15:7). Welcome means that we recognize the dignity of the other person and make room for that person whether that person was anticipated or not, planned or not, convenient or not. This stands in contrast to the concept of "wantedness." When someone is "wanted," they meet some need or expectation of somebody else, and the temptation is to think that their value rises and falls with their degree of "wantedness." Welcome, on the other hand, recognizes that their value is intrinsic to them. They are welcomed whether we want them or not. While some (like Planned Parenthood) say "Every child a wanted child," we say, "Every child (and every person) a welcome child."

We welcome all he welcomes, and are to make room for all he loves, especially the most unwanted, marginalized, burdensome or inconvenient. If we welcome the baby Jesus, we welcome every baby, we welcome his teaching that every life is sacred, and we live accordingly.

Dr. King, in his efforts to advance human rights and equality, taught about *the Beloved Community,* where all were welcomed. We have made great progress, but today all are still not welcomed, particularly the unborn. That is why Dr. King's sister-in-law, Naomi Ruth Barber King (wife of Martin's brother A.D. King), proclaimed in Washington, D.C. in January 2011 the declaration, *The Beloved Community and the Unborn,* in which she referenced his Christmas 1967 sermon and stated, "*In our day, therefore, we cannot ignore the discrimination, injustice, and violence that are being inflicted on the youngest and smallest members of the human family, the children in the womb... We declare today that these children too are members of the Beloved Community, that our destiny is linked with theirs, and that therefore they deserve justice, equality, and protection.*" The full text of the declaration was included in the time capsule that was placed in the monument to Dr. King in Washington.

And with God's grace, the task will be completed, because it is a task fueled by the power of love. Christ gives us the power to welcome all whom he welcomes. His yoke is easy, his burden light.

As we celebrate Christmas, let's echo Dr. King's words, as well as those of Naomi King, and let's pray this beautiful prayer written by our former pastoral associate and current EWTN host, Jim Pinto:

# FACE PRAYER

Heavenly Father,
I embrace your grace this day,
So that I might not:
Think of another,
Speak to another or
Touch another,
Without first looking for
Your Face in the other.
I ask all this through
Jesus Christ:
God Incarnate,
God with Skin,
God made Poor,
God with a Face. Amen!

# THE POLITICAL MEANING OF CHRISTMAS

Christmas, surprisingly enough, is quite political.

In the pagan view of government, the law came from the mouth of the king and the people counted for nothing. They had neither input nor recourse against those who ruled over them. There were no elections, no lobbying, no opportunity to change the law or those who made it.

But when the Lord Jesus came, he taught that people are called to be sons and daughters of God, and therefore they *do* count. He opened the way for us all to share the divine nature. And if that is true, then no public official can dominate or own other people; no legislator or governor, Congress or Court, can have a veto power over human rights! Thanks to Christmas, *everyone counts*, and therefore everyone *has a voice*. Power and authority become service; government becomes representative; legislators become ministers of God (see Romans 13) and are accountable to him, and issues matter only because people matter more.

This is why we can elect our leaders, and lobby them once they are in office. This is why Christians have a political responsibility.

Some still doubt whether the pulpit is the place to talk about elections. But in fact, *if there were no pulpits, neither would there be any elections*. The problem is not that the Church is becoming too political; the problem is that our politics have become too pagan. And it is Christmas that contains the key to changing that!

St. Pope John Paul II marked his pontificate by repeating the most frequent admonition of Scripture: Be not afraid! It doesn't just mean, "Don't worry, have courage." It means that we are called to welcome Jesus Christ and not be afraid that he is going to deprive us of what we long for or restrict our freedom or enslave our hopes. No, welcoming the Savior is precisely the fulfillment of our hopes, the foundation of our freedom, and the heart and soul of our politics!

# NO ROOM IN THE INN

"She wrapped him in swaddling clothes and laid him in a manger, because there was no room for them in the inn" (Luke 2:7).

The fact that there was no room for Jesus, Mary and Joseph in the inn at Bethlehem on the first Christmas should make us wonder, because the birth of Christ was foreseen and planned by God from all eternity. Hundreds of years before it happened, the prophets announced he would be born of a virgin (Is. 7:14) and that Bethlehem would be his birthplace (Micah 5:2). Many other details of his life and death were also foretold. Did God, then, forget to make room for his only son? How is it possible there was no room, when the child born at Christmas owns the inn, and Bethlehem, and the world, and every inch of room in the whole universe?

Obviously, God did this on purpose. There was no room in the inn, because this demonstrates that the world has rejected God. The world makes no room for the God who created it. There was no room in the inn because God wanted to show that his son comes as a Savior, to reconcile a world that is at enmity with God. Being turned away from the inn foreshadows the fact that the Savior himself will be rejected, despised, and ultimately crucified, and that all this was part of God's plan from all eternity. Ultimately, the lack of room in the inn symbolizes the lack of room we make for him in our hearts. When our hearts are filled with all kinds of other desires than God, we gradually crowd him out altogether.

No room at the inn also means that we fail to make room for our brothers and sisters. The first great commandment is to love God, and the second is like it: Love your neighbor as yourself. Christ willed to be left out, because he is always in solidarity with those who are left out, shut out and crowded out. That is the position of the unborn children today. They are crowded out of the busy schedules of so many people doing so many good and important things, but who don't have a finger to lift to protect the lives of these children from abortion. They are crowded out of legislative agendas, preaching schedules, career plans, pastoral plans, and volunteer activities. There's just too much going on already; there's no room in the inn.

Christ comes at Christmas to change all that. Today, he does not seek an inn; he seeks room in our own hearts and lives. And he asks that as we welcome him, we welcome everyone whom he welcomes, including the children most defenseless and forgotten. We welcome the Divine Child, and in doing so, we welcome every child. As we celebrate Christmas, we sing in "O Holy Night" the words, "Chains shall he break, for the slave is our brother, and in his name all oppression shall cease." Amen! Let oppression cease and let Christmas come for the unborn!

# THE EMPTY MANGER

During Advent, Christians gather around the Manger, as yet empty. "Come, Lord Jesus, do not delay," the Church's liturgy prays.

Just as the baby in the Manger represents for us the greatest gift God brings, so the emptiness of the Manger represents the deep needs of the human heart -- needs that not only we experience individually, but that the human family has experienced from the beginning of time.

Adam and Eve alienated themselves and their descendants from intimacy with God. They lost paradise, and ever since, humanity has longed to regain it. The Manger has been empty.

As much as we need food, we need *meaning* just as much. We want to know who God is and what life is about. The human mind can only go so far in figuring it out; we need the God who speaks, and he spoke in full measure only when Christ came. Until then, the Manger was empty.

And humanity needed to be reconciled to God. Isaac asked his father Abraham, as they walked to the place of sacrifice, "*The fire and wood are here, but where is the lamb for the burnt offering?*" (Gen. 22:7). Indeed, where is the lamb? What sacrifice can suffice for our sins? How can we overcome the enmity that separates us from God? Who will be the bridge back to paradise? The Manger was still empty.

Humanity, moreover, awaited the fulfillment of the great promise that death itself would be conquered. Humanity awaited one who could free all people from the fear that death would be the end of the human story. "*He will destroy the veil that veils all peoples, the web that is woven over all nations; he will destroy death forever*" (Isaiah 25:7-8). This has been the hope of the human heart from the beginning. But the Manger was still empty.

Empty, that is, until the Holy Night in Bethlehem. Hence, we sing, *"The hopes and fears of all the years are met in Thee tonight" (from the hymn "O Little Town of Bethlehem).*

His birth is all about hope fulfilled and hope inspired. He is the one who answers all our questions, fulfills all our hopes, and calms all our fears.

In him we welcome the Culture of Life. It has been said that the false god transforms suffering into violence, but the true God transforms violence into suffering. In the newborn Christ, we find the God in whom we can resist the temptation to solve an unexpected pregnancy by the violence of abortion, or a terminal illness by the violence of euthanasia.

Instead, we can treasure every life, including our own, and transform suffering into loving service.

As we place the statue of the Baby Jesus into the Manger scene on Christmas morning, let us embrace the hope he brings, and work to fulfill the vision of peace, life and love that Christmas inspires.

# THE CRIB AND THE BLOOD

There is no crib without the cross. The Servant Songs of the prophet Isaiah foretell that Jesus will be "a man of sorrows, acquainted with grief" (Is. 53:3), and even from his presentation at the temple, the prophet Simeon tells Mary that he will be "a sign that will be opposed" (Lk.2:34). After all, Jesus took on a human body precisely so he could offer it on the cross.

The liturgical calendar brings home to us this unavoidable juxtaposition of the birth of Christ, and of bloodshed for him. The day after Christmas is the Feast of Saint Stephen, the first follower of Christ to willingly sacrifice his life for him. We read of him in the Acts of the Apostles (see chapters 6 and 7). Then, two days later, we have the Feast of the Holy Innocents. We read that upon being told by the Magi that Jesus had been born, King Herod "and all Jerusalem" were greatly troubled, leading to Herod's selfish and barbaric decree to slaughter all the infants of two years age and younger in and around Bethlehem (see Matthew chapter 2).

The light came into the world, but some – like the killers of these Holy Innocents and the killers of St. Stephen – preferred darkness to light, because their deeds were evil (see John 3:19-21). So it will always be. The light brings unity and peace – for those who accept it. It also brings division and conflict – because some will always reject it. There can be no crib without the cross. There can be no Christmas without martyrdom.

And this indeed brings us back to the identity of the baby: The one who is born is "Messiah ***and Lord"*** (Lk. 2:11). That means he is the one to whom we owe absolute loyalty, even above life itself. He is God.

And he is the God who gives life. The slaughter of the Innocents, in particular, has a parallel in today's tragedy of abortion. Herod was motivated by fear of how this newborn King would deprive him of power, just as the King of Egypt, in Exodus chapter one, ordered the slaughter of the Hebrew children for fear that they would grow too numerous. It's amazing how powerful kings can be so afraid of babies. But that fear permeates our culture and fuels abortion: We fear what the child will demand of us, and how the child will deprive us of freedom or other resources. Fear makes us forget that it is precisely in pushing ourselves out of the way to make room for new life that we find our own fulfillment and happiness.

Indeed, the wisdom of the cross is expressed in the adage that the false god transforms suffering into violence, but the true God transforms violence into suffering. And that happens through the power of love, found in the cross, and before it, in the crib.

# CHRISTMAS: JUST LIKE EASTER

I remember as a young boy going into Church for Mass one Easter Sunday when it was snowing! The pastor welcomed the congregation at the outset by saying, "Merry Christmas!"

Actually, his humorous greeting points to a serious and substantive link between Christmas and Easter that goes far beyond an occasional similarity in the weather. In fact, they are intimately connected. *Christmas, in fact, is for the purpose of Easter.*

Jesus took on a human body at the Incarnation precisely so he could offer the sacrifice of that body upon the cross, and take that human nature through the crucible of death into the glory of the Resurrection.

"A body you have prepared for me … I come to do your will," the Psalmist writes.

The angels on Christmas night proclaimed, "Glory to God in the highest, and on earth, peace to men of good will."

What is the glory of God? Saint Irenaeus of Lyons answers that in his celebrated definition: *"Man, living man, is the glory of God."* And it is precisely in Jesus Christ, crucified and risen from the dead, that man becomes fully alive, that his natural life is clothed with the divine nature and given a share in life eternal.

The coming of Christ at Christmas is the first step to leading us to that fullness of life. Jesus come down from heaven to lead us up to heaven; Christmas is, if you will, the grasping of our hand; Easter is the pulling us up to where he is. It is all one great act of divine intervention and salvation.

"Glory to God in the highest, and on earth, peace…" This is the source of our peace. The Risen Christ showed the disciples his hands and feet, and said, "Peace be with you." The Christmas announcement of peace is the promise that the Easter announcement of peace fulfills. God is glorified because human life will now be glorified by being freed from the kingdom of death and transferred into Christ's kingdom of light.

Peace is not just the absence of war. Peace does not reign in a city just because no bombs are falling or tanks rolling through the streets. Peace is the fullness of life, and the perfection of relationships. It is the security of justice and the fulfillment of God's plan for each person.

Peace is lost long before guns are fired. It is lost as soon as one person's human rights are violated, or one life is trampled. A neighborhood might appear peaceful, but if an abortion mill is operating in it, there is no peace, because innocent blood is being shed.

That's why the reality of what Christmas and Easter bring us -- the saving presence and action of Christ -- both impel and oblige us to actively oppose injustice and build peace by defending human rights, starting with life itself.

That is also why Christmas and Easter are marked by joy. Joy does not mean that everything is going just as we prefer or that we have all we want. The world can be falling apart around us, but the joy we have as Christians is the joy of knowing that God is with us, that we rely only on him, that he is all we need, and that no power on earth or in hell can separate us from him. That is the meaning of "Merry Christmas." We may lose health or loved ones or possessions or positions -- but we do not lose God, in whom ultimately we receive everything.

Christmas peace is the promise of Easter redemption, when human life is exalted rather than trampled. May our celebration of these feasts proclaim the Glory of God, and fill us with his peace!

# THE ADVENT - CHRISTMAS SEASON: FEASTS, PRACTICES, AND PRAYERS

Christmas is always observed on December 25. One explanation for why is that the Romans of antiquity celebrated on that day the "Feast of the Unconquered Sun," because, as we also know, around December 21 we have the shortest amount of daylight of the year, and then, after that "winter solstice," the amount of sunlight begins to increase again. So the sun has not been conquered. Christians, therefore, made it a celebration of the unconquered Son of God, the light who came into the world. The light shines on in the darkness, a darkness that has not overcome it (see John 1:4-5).

The precursor of Jesus, John the Baptist, said, **"He must increase, while I must decrease."** Interestingly, John's birthday is celebrated on June 24 (because we know from **Luke** that when Mary conceived Jesus, her cousin Elizabeth was already in her sixth month of pregnancy with John). That date happens to be right around the summer solstice, the day with the most sunlight, and after that day the light begins to decrease until Jesus comes.

The four Sundays before Christmas are the four Sundays of Advent, (for the Latin word for "coming") a season that marks the beginning of the Church's liturgical year. This season, as some of the essays here explain, focus on his coming both at the end of time, and also in his Incarnation and Birth.

The Advent season is about the coming of the Light of the World (see John 9:5), Jesus Christ. This is why the "Advent wreath" with its candles is such a common tradition. The wreath is a circle, signifying the eternity of the Son of God: there is no beginning and no end. As Advent progresses, an additional one of the four candles is lit, bringing more light.

The Third Sunday of Advent is called "Gaudete (Latin for "Rejoice") Sunday," given the closeness of Christmas, and candle is a rose color. The other Advent candles, as well as the liturgical vestments of Advent, are purple, because that's the color of the sky as it transitions each morning from darkness to dawn.

Within Advent, the Church calendar observes a number of other feast days that have a special connection with the coming of Christ. One of the major ones is the Immaculate Conception, on December 8. This is the conception ***of Mary in the womb of her mother, St. Anne.*** Mary, chosen from all eternity to be the Mother of God (Jesus), is ***preserved from sin (that is, immaculate),*** precisely because she will have God himself growing in her body. She is, of course, saved through Jesus, as we all are, but in a unique way.

This season also brings us the celebration of Mary as Our Lady of Guadalupe, patroness of the unborn. Mary in that apparition is pregnant with Jesus. One of the essays in this book explains the further meaning of that.

We transition from the Advent season to the Christmas season on Christmas Eve. We are used to singing

Christmas songs all through Advent, so it's easy to miss the significance of this transition. Now comes the Holy Night when, in the middle of the night, God's Word, Jesus Christ, leapt down from heaven (see Wisdom 18:14-15, which is why we have the Mass at Midnight). So now we can sing, "Christ the Savior is Born." Up to now, the prayers and songs ask him to come; now we rejoice that he ***has*** come.

Many are tempted, of course, to think that Christmas is over on December 26. But it has actually just begun. Christmas is a whole season, lasting approximately three weeks, until the Feast of the Baptism of the Lord. During these weeks, there are several key celebrations that look at the Incarnation from several different vantage points. It's like a scene on which a spotlight will focus now on one part and now on the other.

Christmas Eve and Day, of course, bring us into the actual announcement and event of Jesus' miraculous birth, on which we continue to reflect in the following days. As one of the essays in this book explains, the joy of that birth is immediately confronted with the reality of martyrdom, as the first martyr, St. Stephen, has his feast on December 26, and then on December 28 is the Feast of the Holy Innocents. The God who is born for us requires total devotion, even to the giving of one's life.

Within the first eight days of the Christmas season (the "Octave," as it's called), there is also the Feast of the Holy Family. The spotlight is on Jesus, Mary and Joseph ***as a family.*** Jesus made himself like us, grew up with Mary and Joseph, and was obedient to them. Life and family go together.

A week after Christmas (the day that is called the "Octave of Christmas") is New Year's Day, but the liturgical feast of that day is the Solemnity of Mary, the Mother of God. Now the spotlight is on her, individually, as known by her most basic, biblical, and important title. Jesus is God, the Second Person of the Trinity; Mary is therefore literally the Mother of God, even though her Son existed for all eternity before her.

As the Christmas season continues, we come, on the Sunday after the New Year, to the Epiphany. Though linked historically to January 6, the date of this Feast varies. It is a day rich in meaning. "Epiphany" means a "manifestation." It asks, "What child is this?" It shows that this child is Divine, that he is a King. Therefore the Magi from the East bring him gold, frankincense and myrrh, representing the fact that he is a King, that he is God, and that he will sacrifice his life. The Epiphany includes a reference to two other later events that manifest who Jesus is: The wedding feast at Cana, where he "revealed his glory" (John 2:11), and his baptism at the Jordan, where the Dove and the Father's voice showed he is the Son of God.

The Church continues meditating on all these things for another week until the Feast of the Baptism of the Lord. Though also an aspect of the Epiphany, this feast puts the focus more deeply on this event, which marks the beginning of the public ministry of Jesus. That Feast is the conclusion of the Christmas season. We should keep our decorations up until then if at all possible, so that we can reflect, with our senses as well as our minds, on the deep mystery of the Incarnation and all that it brings us.

# AN ADVENT PRAYER FOR LIFE

*(We invite you to say this prayer throughout the Advent season. You will find this and other seasonal prayers related to the pro-life cause at* ***www.PrayerCampaign.org.****)*

God of Life,
We rejoice in the promise of your coming

You have sent your Son, born in Bethlehem.
He is the Prince of Peace, and
The one in whose name all oppression shall cease.

May we welcome his coming each day
And prepare for his coming at the end of time.
May we build a culture that welcomes him
By welcoming every child, born and unborn.

We pray through the same Christ our Lord.
Amen.

# A CHRISTMAS PRAYER FOR LIFE

Glory to God in the Highest!
And peace to His people on earth!

Lord, I thank you for the great
Christmas Gift you bring!
You share in my human nature,
And I share in your Divine nature!

Lord, in your Incarnation,
You have united every human being,
Born and unborn,
To yourself.

In welcoming you, may I welcome them,
serve them, love them.
And may I always defend the children in the womb
And defend their right to be born!

Glory to you, the Newborn King, who live and
reign forever and ever. Amen!

# About the Author and Priests for Life

Read and listen to more of Fr. Frank's reflections on Advent and Christmas at

***www.PriestsForLife.org/Christmas***

**Fr. Frank Pavone** is one of the most prominent pro-life leaders in the world. He was appointed in 1993 by Cardinal John O'Connor to serve as National Director of Priests for Life, and has served as an official of the Vatican's Pontifical Council for the Family and a member of the Vatican's Pontifical Academy for Life.

**Priests for Life** is one of the world's largest and most prominent organizations focused on ending abortion. It is a family of ministries, including Rachel's Vineyard, the Silent No More Awareness Campaign, Deacons for Life, Seminarians for Life, Missionaries of the Gospel of Life, Hispanic Outreach, Civil Rights for the Unborn, PoliticalResponsibility.com, PrayerCampaign.org, StandTrue Youth Outreach, and much more.



Tune in to our daily broadcasts at ***EndAbortion.TV***.

Receive free pro-life commentary from Fr. Frank.
Request it at ***subscribe@priestsforlife.org***.

Priests for Life is supported only by people like you!
Please help our work at ***www.prolifedonation.com***.

**Priests for Life**

PO Box 236695 • Cocoa, FL 32923

321-500-1000

***mail@priestsforlife.org***

***www.EndAbortion.US***

# PROLIFESOCIALMEDIA.COM

Connect with us on social media so we can exchange encouragement and information.

At ***www.ProLifeSocialMedia.com***, you will find a multitude of platforms that Priests for Life manages. Follow us, friend us, like us, and communicate with us. Among our largest platforms are the following:

Truth Social @FrFrankPavone

Gettr.com/user/frfrankpavone
Gettr.com/user/JanetMorana

Tiktok.com/@frfrankpavone

Rumble.com/user/FrFrankPavone

Youtube.com/FrFrankpavone

Facebook.com/FatherFrankPavone
Facebook.com/SilentNoMoreJanet

Twitter: @FrFrankPavone
Twitter: @JanetMorana

Instagram.com/FrFrankPavone
Instagram.com/JanetMorana

Soundcloud.com/Priests-for-Life

Parler.com/#/user/FrFrankPavone

Linkedin.com/in/FatherFrankPavone

Pinterest.com/PriestsForLife